The No Kids Club

Written by
William Anthony

Illustrated by
Rosie Groom

THE
NO KIDS
CLUB

"Are we all in?" said Erin. The kids sat down.

The No Kids Club

INTRO TO
PHASE 5

/ie/

Level 4+
Blue+

BookLife

Helpful Hints for Reading at Home

The graphemes (written letters) and phonemes (units of sound) used throughout this series are aligned with Letters and Sounds. This offers a consistent approach to learning whether reading at home or in the classroom.

THIS BLUE+ BOOK BAND SERVES AS AN INTRODUCTION TO PHASE 5. EACH BOOK IN THIS BAND USES ALL PHONEMES LEARNED UP TO PHASE 4, WHILE INTRODUCING ONE PHASE 5 PHONEME. HERE IS A LIST OF PHONEMES FOR THIS PHASE, WITH THE NEW PHASE 5 PHONEME. AN EXAMPLE OF THE PRONUNCIATION CAN BE FOUND IN BRACKETS.

Phase 3			
j (jug)	v (van)	w (wet)	x (fox)
y (yellow)	z (zoo)	zz (buzz)	qu (quick)
ch (chip)	sh (shop)	th (thin/then)	ng (ring)
ai (rain)	ee (feet)	igh (night)	oa (boat)
oo (boot/look)	ar (farm)	or (for)	ur (hurt)
ow (cow)	oi (coin)	ear (dear)	air (fair)
ure (sure)	er (corner)		

New Phase 5 Phoneme	ie (spies, lies, pies.)

HERE ARE SOME WORDS WHICH YOUR CHILD MAY FIND TRICKY.

Phase 4 Tricky Words			
said	were	have	there
like	little	so	one
do	when	some	out
come	what		

TOP TIPS FOR HELPING YOUR CHILD TO READ:

• Allow children time to break down unfamiliar words into units of sound and then encourage children to string these sounds together to create the word.

• Encourage your child to point out any focus phonics when they are used.

• Read through the book more than once to grow confidence.

• Ask simple questions about the text to assess understanding.

• Encourage children to use illustrations as prompts.

INTRO TO PHASE 5

/ie/

This book introduces the phoneme /ie/ and is a Blue+ Level 4+ book band.

"We are all at this Spies for Lies meeting for one thing," she said.

"To be proper spies and stop the lies of all mums and dads," said Erin.

"They lie and then creep off. We must track down what they creep off to do."

The Spies for Lies all went off with plans.

Meg left a camcorder in a pie. "This will get them," she said.

Al set up a recorder on his dad's tie.
"This is good," he said.

Craig stuck a tracker on his mum's magpie chain. "Yes!" he said.

At the next Spies for Lies meeting,
the kids took a look at the proof.

SPIES FOR LIES

PROOF!

Meg's camcorder got her mum's lie.
Mum said she had to go to Saturn.

REC

00:00:06:28

"Saturn? Do they think we are fools?" cried Tom from the back.

Al's recorder got his mum and dad's lie.
They said they had to go to jail.

TIE RECORDING 01

0:07

2:30

"Jail?" cried Ella. "Al's mum and dad are good – they will never go to jail."

Craig had tried hard, but there had not been a beep on his tracker... yet.

Beep! Beep! Beep! The tracker went off.
"Mum is off!" said Craig.

"We can go with her," said Erin.
The Spies for Lies ran.

Craig's mum was on an odd street.
"Wait until she is in," said Erin.

The Spies for Lies ran down the street.
There was a placard.

THE
NO KIDS
CLUB

"The No Kids Club?" said Erin. "What is that?"

The kids burst in. They had a big shock.

The door sign reads: THE NO KIDS CLUB

It was a fun room, but it had lots of mums and dads and no kids!

There was a pool to splish and splash and a pit to jump in.

"Stop!" cried Erin. "You lied to us to act like kids. But you are adults!"

Erin was right. The mums and dads left to go and be adults.

Erin got a pen to claim the fun room for the kids.

The
NO KIDS
CLUB

"This will now be The Kids Club!" said Erin.

The No Kids Club

1)   Who are the Spies for Lies and what do they do?

2)   Where do the Spies for Lies find all the mums and dads?

3)   What does Meg hide her camcorder in?
      a) A wall

      b) A pie

      c) A tie

4)   Is it ever OK to tell a lie? Why?

5)   How do you think the children felt when they took over The No Kids Club?

During reading

Remind your child of what they know and what they can do independently. If reading aloud, support your child if they hesitate or ask for help by telling the word. If reading to themselves, remind your child that they can come and ask for your help if stuck.

After reading

Support comprehension by asking your child to tell you about the story. Use the story order puzzle to encourage your child to retell the story in the right sequence, in their own words. The correct sequence can be found on the next page.

Help your child think about the messages in the book that go beyond the story and ask: "Why do you think Puss found it so easy to trick the giant?" Give your child a chance to respond to the story: "Did you have a favourite part? Did you like the ending of the story?"

Extending learning

Help your child understand the story structure by using the same sentence patterning and adding different elements. "Let's make up a new story about Puss. What might he want this time, and what plan might he come up with to get what he wants?"

In the classroom, your child's teacher may be teaching use of punctuation marks. Ask your child to identify some question marks and exclamation marks in the story and then ask them to practise reading each of the whole sentences with appropriate expression.

Franklin Watts
First published in Great Britain in 2021
by The Watts Publishing Group

Copyright © The Watts Publishing Group 2021

Series Editors: Jackie Hamley and Melanie Palmer
Series Advisors: Dr Sue Bodman and Glen Franklin
Series Designers: Peter Scoulding and Cathryn Gilbert

A CIP catalogue record for this book is
available from the British Library.

ISBN 978 1 4451 7400 6 (hbk)
ISBN 978 1 4451 7401 3 (pbk)
ISBN 978 1 4451 7402 0 (library ebook)
ISBN 978 1 4451 8151 6 (ebook)

Printed in China

Franklin Watts
An imprint of
Hachette Children's Group
Part of The Watts Publishing Group
Carmelite House
50 Victoria Embankment
London EC4Y 0DZ

An Hachette UK Company
www.hachette.co.uk

www.franklinwatts.co.uk

FSC
www.fsc.org
MIX
Paper from
responsible sources
FSC® C104740

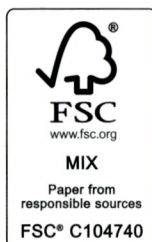

Answer to Story order: 3, 1, 4, 5, 2